Gregor Mendel Genetics Pioneer

Lynn Van Gorp, M.S.

Life Science Readers: Gregor Mendel: Genetics Pioneer

Publishing Credits

Editorial Director
Dona Herweck Rice

Associate Editor
Joshua BishopRoby

Editor-in-Chief
Sharon Coan, M.S.Ed.

Creative Director
Lee Aucoin

Illustration Manager
Timothy J. Bradley

Publisher
Rachelle Cracchiolo, M.S.Ed.

Science Contributor
Sally Ride Science™

Science Consultants
Thomas R. Ciccone, B.S., M.A.Ed.,
Chino Hills High School
Dr. Ronald Edwards,
DePaul University

Teacher Created Materials
5301 Oceanus Drive
Huntington Beach, CA 92649
http://www.tcmpub.com

ISBN 978-0-7439-0598-5

Printed by: 51497
Printed in: China

Table of Contents

Gregor Johann Mendel

Johann Mendel (YOH-hahn MEN-dl) was born in 1822 into a poor farming family. He was born in the Austrian Empire, in a town that is now in the Czech (CHEK) Republic.

When Mendel grew up, he became a monk. He was also a **botanist.** A botanist is a scientist who studies plants. Mendel experimented with garden peas. People say he is the father of modern **genetics** because of his work.

a view of Prague in the Czech Republic

Czech Republic

The Czech Republic is in Europe. It is in between Germany, Austria, and Poland. It is a small country. It is smaller than the state of South Carolina. Its capital city is Prague.

Mendel's life was hard. He worked as a gardener when he was young, but he wanted a better life. It was almost impossible for poor people to get a good education. His parents helped pay for him to go to school. Then his father got hurt. After that, his two sisters helped Mendel. To continue his education, Mendel entered a **monastery**. It was a teaching monastery. It was a place for learning and scientific inquiry. There, Mendel was given the name Gregor (GREG-er).

Monasteries such as this one in Greece have been centers of learning for centuries.

This is the monastery where Mendel lived.

Monasteries

There are monasteries all over the world. Monks and nuns live in them. They spend time praying and meditating there. The monks of Mendel's monastery belonged to the Augustinian (aw-guhs-TIN-ee-in) order.

Many well-known scientists lived in monasteries. People throughout time have often gone to monasteries to learn. Some do research and teach there. Monasteries also often give shelter to travelers and to the poor.

A Teacher First, Then a Scientist

Mendel is in the back row of this group of monks and teachers from 1865.

Mendel lived at the monastery. He became a priest when he was 25 years old. He got up every morning at six. He went straight to the library to study. He studied many sciences. He also taught Latin, Greek, and math to other students. He took a test to become an official teacher, but he did not pass it. So, he went to the University of Vienna to get his teaching diploma. He studied for two years.

Mendel was very sick when he took his tests. Once again, he did not pass them. He decided to withdraw from the school. But even though he did not pass, he had learned valuable research skills.

Test Anxiety

When Mendel went to take his tests, he became ill. It is thought that he had test anxiety. He was so scared of taking the tests, he couldn't even take them. Many people have test anxiety.

the University of Vienna

Mendel couldn't teach any longer. He had to do something else for work. At the university, he liked the work of a biologist there named Frank Unger. Biologists study the science of life and living things. Unger had a different view of **inheritance**. He looked at nature. He saw similarities and differences in the way animals and plants grew. Mendel had seen the same things when he was working on the family farm.

Genetics

Reproduction is the process by which offspring are created. Each species reproduces its own kind. In other words, people make people. Dogs make dogs. Trees make trees. Reproduction is needed for a species to survive.

When living things reproduce, they pass their genetic material to their offspring. This material is what makes a living thing what it is. It is found in the cells of living things.

In the center of cells are **chromosomes**. Chromosomes are made of **genes**. In a human being, there are 23 pairs of chromosomes in each cell. Each chromosome holds thousands of genes. **Traits** pass from parent to offspring by way of these genes.

People get their genes from both their birth parents. A person's body follows the instructions given by the genes. These instructions tell the body everything, from what the person's eye color should be to how big his or her feet should grow.

People get their hair color, among other things, from their birth parents.

The same is true for other animals and plants. The parent passes its traits to the offspring, whether the offspring is a cow, monkey, pineapple, or elm tree.

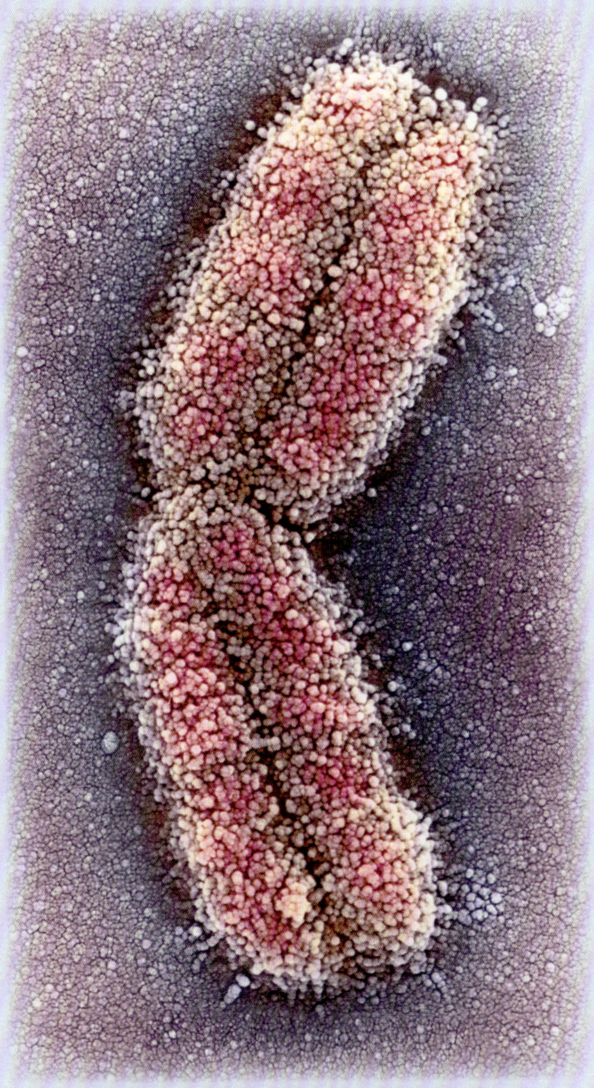

Chromosomes are so small that they can only be seen when they bunch together like this.

DNA

A baby's first cell has a code in it. The code has the instructions needed to make that baby. That first cell has little bits inside called chromosomes. Half these chromosomes come from the mother's egg cell. Half come from the father's sperm cell. The major part of all chromosomes is called **DNA**. DNA carries a person's genetic information or code.

Genes

Genes determine the color of animals' coats. Many genes interact to make the color. That's why there are so many different color patterns in cats, dogs, and other animals.

Mendel Studies Garden Peas

Mendel's father **bred** fruit trees. Mendel helped his father when he was young. That interest stayed with him. He wasn't allowed to teach biology. But he could do research.

It was not possible for Mendel to study fruit trees. So he studied other plants. He decided to research the common pea. He grew them in his garden. They were easy to raise. They had a short breeding time. *Breeding* is another word for reproduction. Best of all, the peas could be **cross-pollinated**. That means that one variety could be bred with another.

Mendel bought seeds from people who lived in the area. Peas were a popular vegetable at that time. Many types were available. Mendel is said to have started with 34 different varieties of pea plants. Over time, he grew and tested at least 28,000 pea plants in his gardens.

Interesting to See
An illustration from the Album Benary (1876–1893) shows some of the characteristics of pea plants that Mendel studied.

Eugenics

Many people oversimplified Mendel's findings. They thought it would be easy to change people's traits. Many countries wanted to improve the majority race that lived in them. They thought they could breed out traits they didn't like. This is called **eugenics** (yoo-JEN-iks). Nazi Germany killed more than 200,000 people with disabilities. Some of these people were in mental institutions. Others had birth defects. In the end, it didn't work. Genetics is very complicated. It cannot be controlled so easily.

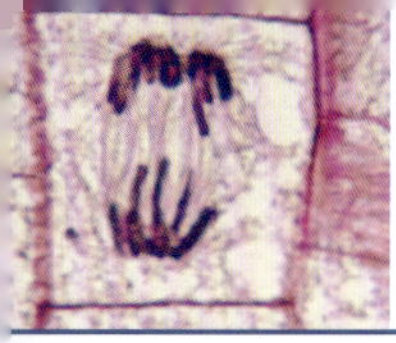

Mendel's Laws of Heredity

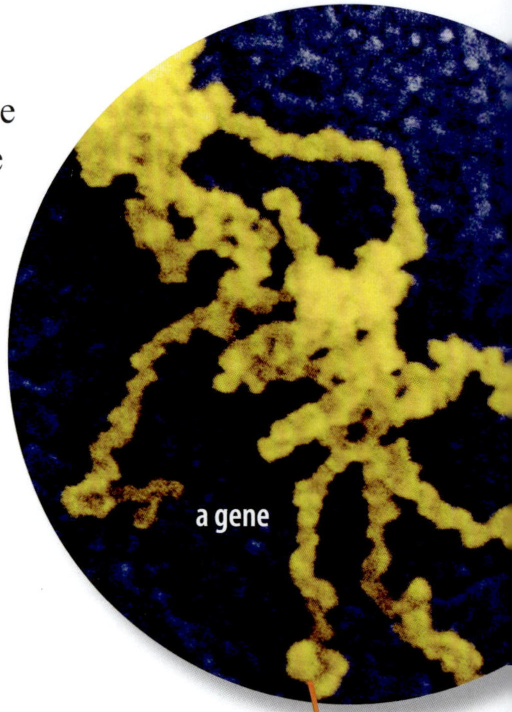

Before Mendel, many people believed in the **theory of blending**. They thought **offspring** would have traits somewhere in between those of their parents. So, if a mother had blue eyes and a father had green eyes, their children would have blue-green eyes. This theory did not explain variations. It also could not explain the differences that occur between species.

Mendel **crossbred,** or mixed, thousands of pea plants. This allowed him to make predictions. These are now called Mendel's Laws of **Heredity**. They explain how traits are passed from generation to generation.

Peas and People

Mendel studied garden peas. Scientists began to see that the concepts he described could be seen in people, too.

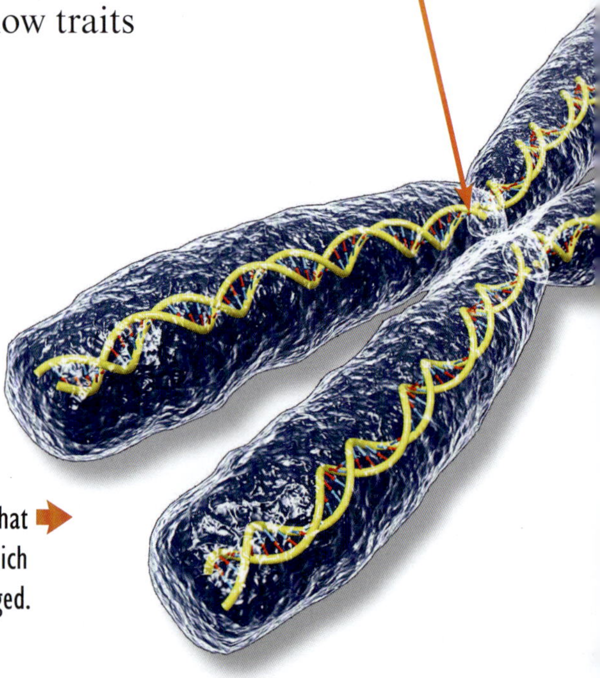

This is a chromosome that contains DNA strands on which genes are arranged.

Eye Color

Eye color is a physical trait. Some parents like to guess what their baby's eye color will be. Eye color is partly determined by the amount of something called *melanin*. It is in the iris of the eye. Brown eyes have a lot of melanin. Blue eyes have very little. Genes control the amount of melanin.

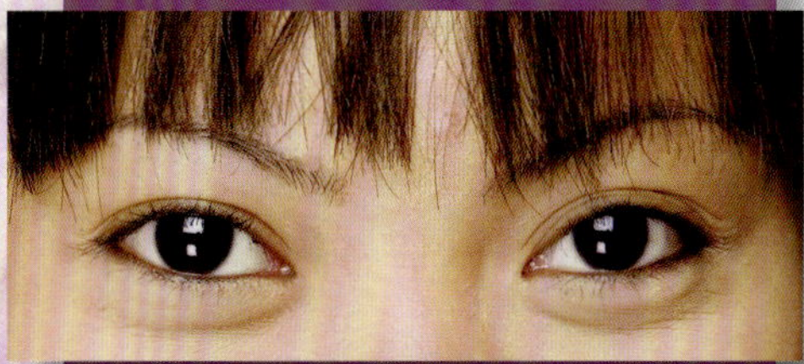

Most of the world's people have dark eyes, ranging from brown to nearly black.

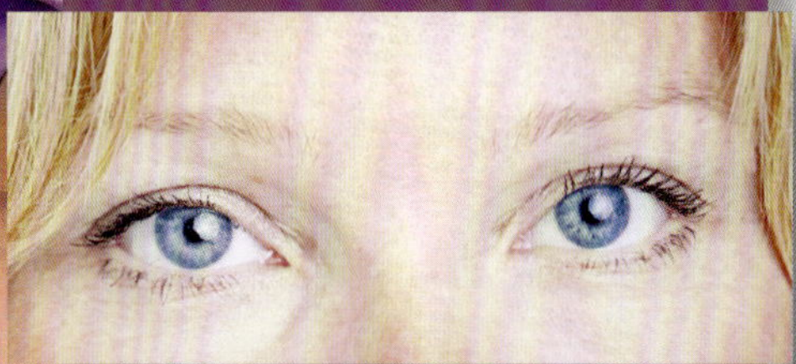

Blue eyes only occur when neither parent gives the baby a brown gene.

Individual traits are inherited in expected or predictable ways. A genetic trait is called a **genotype** (JEE-nuh-tipe). A **phenotype** (FEE-nuh-type) is a trait you can see. It is the result of the interaction between a genotype and the environment. Examples include shape, size, and color.

The traits of the pea plant that this pod comes from include a tall stem, flowers on top, round seeds, green seed color and coat, and a puffed green pod.

Mendel found that some traits show up in offspring without any blending. He looked at seven pairs of seed traits to compare them. Each trait had two phenotypes, or two differences he could see. They were as follows:

- **stem length**—tall or short
- **flower position**—top or side
- **seed shape**—round or wrinkled
- **seed color**—green or yellow
- **flower color**—purple or white
- **pod shape**—puffed or pinched
- **pod color**—green or yellow

More Alike Than Different

Nearly 100 percent of each person's DNA is exactly the same as other people's DNA! Only .1 percent is different. This small difference is why features such as eye and hair color vary. It's also why some people get sick and some have different reactions to medicine. Otherwise, we are very much the same.

Traits Mendel Compared

Character	Dominant Trait	Recessive Trait
stem length	 tall	 short
flower position	 top	 side
seed shape	 round	 wrinkled
seed color	 yellow	 green
flower color	 purple	 white
pod shape	 puffed	 pinched
pod color	 green	 yellow

Dominant and Recessive Genes

Mendel discovered **dominant** and **recessive** genes. He noted the traits of each plant's parents. He controlled how the plants were **fertilized**. He moved the pollen of the flower on one plant to the flower on another plant.

For every trait, each parent passes one gene to its child. The child then has two genes. The genes interact with each other. The mix makes the child's trait.

There are two versions for each gene. The different versions are called **alleles** (uh-LEELS). There is one allele for attached earlobes. There is another allele for unattached earlobes.

Sometimes the child gets two of the same allele. Sometimes the child gets two different ones. If the alleles are different, then one is dominant. The other is recessive. Dominant alleles only need one allele to be seen. Recessive alleles need two to be seen. A recesive gene will only be seen if both parents pass it on.

An example is pod color in pea plants. The green-pod allele is dominant. Peas need only one green-pod allele to be green. The yellow-pod allele is recessive. The plant needs two yellow-pod alleles to be yellow.

Orchid farmers often harvest pollen from one plant to breed it with another.

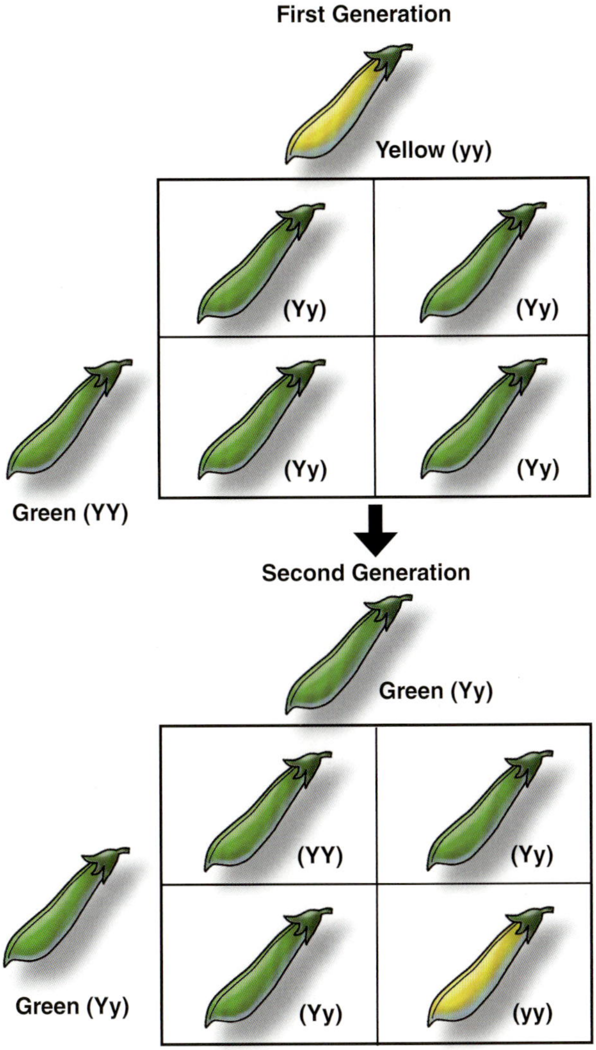

This chart shows the possible allele combinations in two generations of pea pods. The green dominant allele is shown with a capital *Y*. The yellow recessive allele is shown with a lowercase *y*. The pod will be yellow only when it has two recessive alleles.

Allele Colors

These bean pods have different-color gene alleles. One pod color allele is green. The other is yellow. Green is the dominant color.

You can tell that there are different alleles for hair color. These three children have different hair-color alleles. We know that because they have blond, red, and brown hair.

A human example of Mendel's law can be seen in tongue rolling. The ability to roll one's tongue is a dominant trait.

Both parents have two genes that relate to tongue rolling. They got them from their parents. They can have either two dominant genes or two recessive genes. Or they can have one of each. They each pass one of their genes to their child. If a

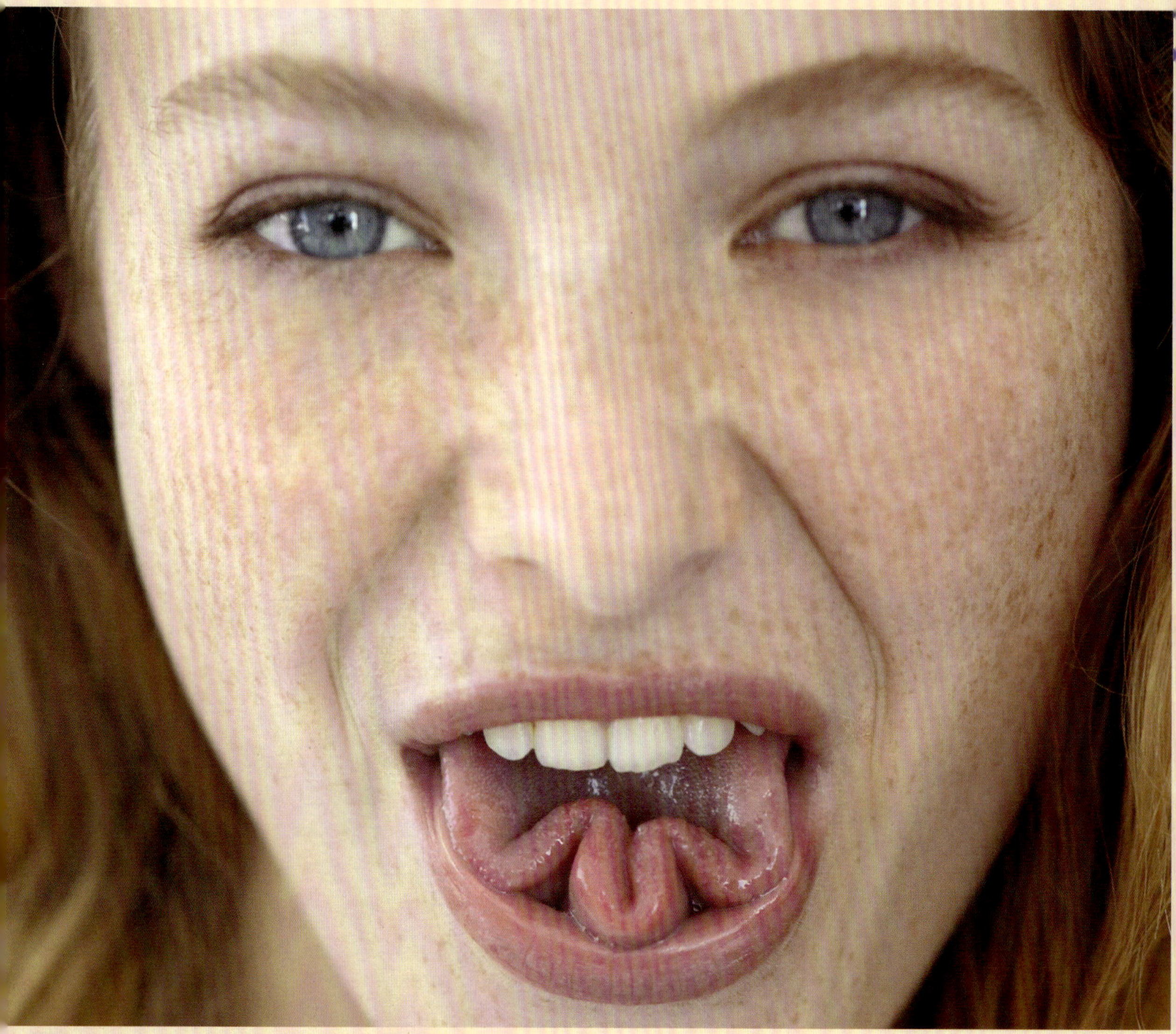

parent has two dominant genes, they will have to pass down a dominant gene. If they have two recessive genes, they will pass down a recessive gene. If they have one of each, though, they might pass down either one. There's no way of telling.

If a child receives one of each gene, the child will be able to roll his or her tongue. The only way the child won't be able to roll it is if he or she receives two recessive genes.

Dominant and Recessive Traits

	Dominant Traits	Recessive Traits
eye color	brown	gray, green, hazel, blue
hair	dark hair	blond, light
	non-red	red
	curly	straight
facial features	dimples	no dimples
	freckles	no freckles

Remember: Both parents need to pass the recessive trait in order to inherit it. Do you have any recessive traits?

◀ Tongue-rolling is a dominant trait.

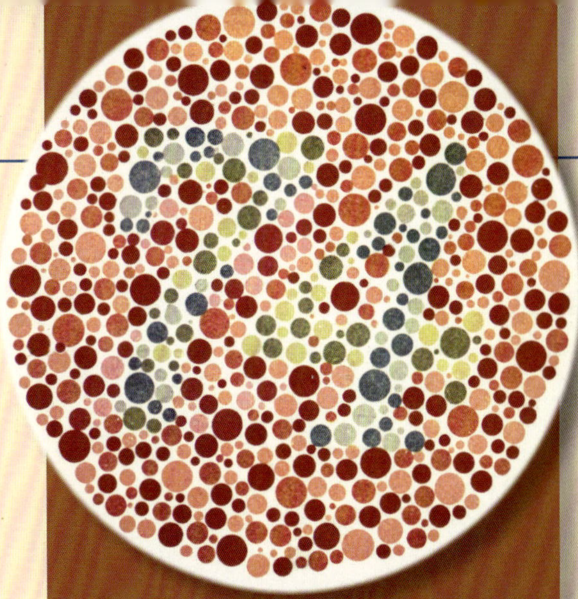

Color Blindness

Color blindness is a genetic condition. People who have it cannot see certain colors. There is no cure for it. About one out of 12 men is color-blind. About one out of 200 women is.

Red/green color blindness is the most common type of color blindness. Someone with normal color vision will see a 74 in the dot pattern above. Someone with red/green color blindness will see a 21 in the pattern or no number at all.

Mendel's Research

Mendel worked very hard. He experimented with thousands of plants. He believed that his experiments would not work if he did not study enough plants. He thought his results might happen by chance, not science. He experimented in his garden for eight years.

Mendel went to a meeting of scientists in 1865. He reported the results of his research. The scientists were polite. But they did not seem to understand the importance of his findings. His research was so different from other work being done at the time. There was very little reaction to his work. No one seemed to notice it. The next year, his report was published. Still, no one seemed to notice.

Unfortunately, Mendel had few opportunities to share his work. It took a long time for people to find out about new research. There were no computers or Internet back then. If there were, maybe Mendel would have been recognized for his work before his death. Perhaps he would have been able to see how important his work would become. In fact, it provided the base for genetic research in the 20th century.

This plant was the result of an experiment that crossed yellow wrinkled peas (top left) with green round peas (top right).

Rosalind Franklin
(1920–1958)

Another scientist who died before people recognized her work was Rosalind Franklin. She produced the first clear photograph of DNA. Sadly, she died of cancer in 1958. She was only 37 years old.

Two other scientists used her photograph as part of their own research. In 1962, they were awarded the **Nobel Prize** for their work in mapping the structure of DNA. Franklin was not mentioned. However, the scientists later acknowledged Franklin's work and its importance to their own. Today the world is well aware of Franklin and the contribution she made to genetics.

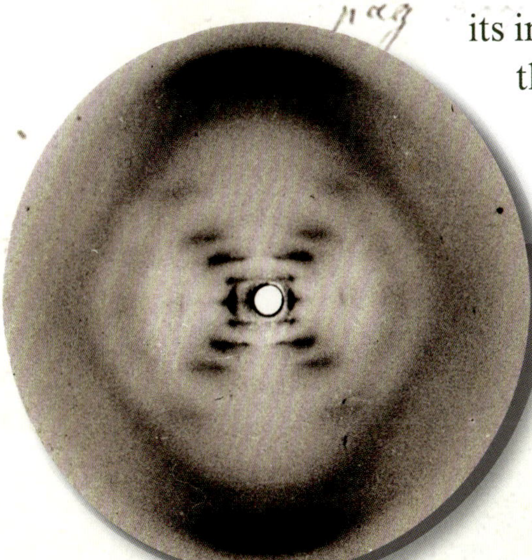

Franklin's photograph of DNA

Mendel's Legacy

Mendel died in 1884 at the age of 62. Few people were aware of his work until the early 1900s. That is when scientists began to understand and think about what he had done.

More than 50 years after Mendel shared his research, another scientist named Hugo De Vries did similar work. Most of the results were similar. He came up with the idea of gene **mutation**. He thought a gene could change and make an instant change in the offspring. He said a mutation would show a change in a single generation. It wouldn't wait until the second generation. He published a book about his theory. It was very controversial. People had strong opinions about his theory.

Since then, other scientists have studied pea plants. Some of their findings back up Mendel's work. Some disagree with Mendel's findings. Scientists today keep studying genes to figure them out. There are still many questions to answer in the study of genes.

Hugo De Vries did similar research to that of Mendel.

Dog Chromosomes

Dogs have more chromosomes than you do! Dogs have 78 chromosomes. You have only 46. Luckily, the number of chromosomes does not relate to how advanced an organism is. Dogs have more chromosomes, but humans have more coding genes than any other species.

Mendel's Microscope

Scientists knew they needed to understand more about how organisms reproduced. They needed to see detailed images of the parts of a cell. So, they needed to use a microscope. Mendel had used a microscope, but it was not powerful enough. He couldn't see the chromosomes, or the parts of a cell that contain the genetic material.

Geneticist: Barbara McClintock

Cold Spring Harbor Laboratory

Jumping Genes

Barbara McClintock never gave up. She spent most of her career growing corn to study genetics. For years, no one believed her conclusions. But she kept going. Her most surprising discovery was a very special gene that can swap places with other genes. Finally, at the age of 81, she won the 1983 Nobel Prize in Medicine!

McClintock had a garden near her laboratory. She planted different kinds of corn so she could breed them and make new types. Some of those plants came from Central and South America, where she loved to travel. She also loved being a teacher. She taught until she died at the age of 90.

Being There

Someone once said it could take McClintock a whole afternoon to answer a person's question. Then, after talking for hours, she would say, "We'd better stop now—you look tired!"

In Her Words

"It might seem unfair to reward a person for having so much pleasure over the years."

McClintock had to sort through many ears of corn.

Lab: Genetic Dominant/Recessive

Let's Experiment

In this lab, you will survey your families and friends. You will find out how many of them display certain dominant or recessive traits. The trait pairs you will survey are the following:

free earlobes	attached earlobes
can roll tongue in a *U* shape	can't roll tongue in a *U* shape
no widow's peak	widow's peak
dark brown eyes	grey, green, or blue eyes
index finger shorter than ring finger	ring finger shorter than index finger
dark hair	light hair
non-red hair	red hair
curly hair	straight hair

Materials

- paper
- pencil
- computer with spreadsheet application and a printer (optional)

Procedure

1 Prepare a genetic dominant/recessive trait survey form. Using each of the categories listed at the top of this page, make a chart. Leave space after each column to tally total numbers. Above the left-hand column, add the title Dominant Traits. Above the right-hand column, add the title Recessive Traits.

Trait Survey

2 Ask your family members and friends which traits they have.

3 Record their responses on your form.

4 Total the number of responses you tallied for each trait.

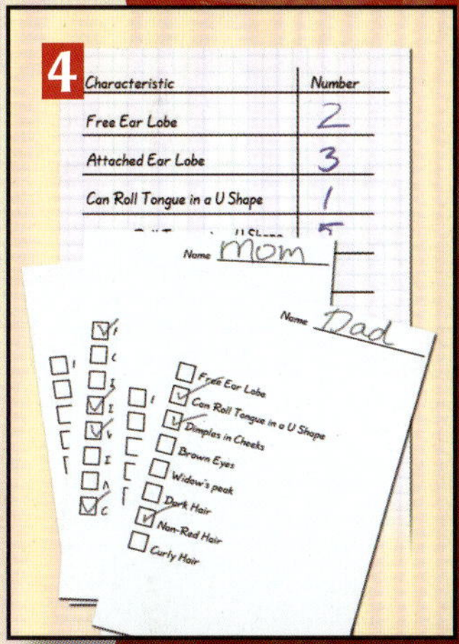

5 Create a bar graph to display your results. If you have them, use a computer and printer to create your graph.

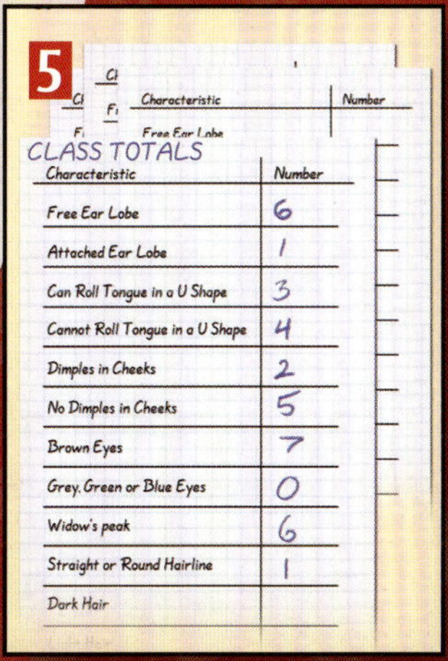

6 Summarize your results.

Conclusion

Dominant traits show up more often than recessive traits. Genetic traits show up in predictable patterns within families. Did you come to the same conclusion?

Extension Idea for Further Study

Use *genetics* as a keyword to research genetic traits on the Internet. Share your most interesting findings by creating a poster.

Glossary

allele—each part of a gene pair

botanist—scientist who studies plant life

bred—kept animals for the purpose of producing offspring in a controlled way

chromosome—a rod-shaped structure in a cell that carries the genes that determine the characteristics an organism inherits from its parents.

crossbreed—to breed new plants or animals from genetically different individuals

cross-pollinated—having the pollen from one plant's flower transferred to another's flower, allowing the genetic traits to mix in their offspring

DNA—a twisted double strand that is the major part of chromosomes and carries genetic information

dominant trait—a trait that appears to mask or hide other traits

eugenics—science that attempts to improve the human race

fertilize—to put a natural or chemical substance on land in order to make plants grow well

gene—a part of a cell's DNA that contains information in a pattern received by each living thing from its parents, and which controls its physical development, behavior, etc.

genetics—a branch of science dealing with heredity and genetic variations

genotype—the genetic makeup of an organism, as opposed to its visible characteristics

heredity—the complete set of inherited characteristics of an organism; the passing on of genetic factors from one generation to the next

inheritance—transmission of traits or qualities from parent to offspring

monastery—a building in which monks and sometimes nuns and priests live and worship

mutation—a change in a gene resulting in a new trait or characteristic that can be inherited, and that can be beneficial, neutral, or harmful in its effect

Nobel Prize—award given each year for achievement in chemistry, literature, physics, physiology or medicine, economics, and world peace

offspring—the descendants of people, animals, and plants

phenotype—the visible characteristics of an organism, resulting from the interaction between its genes and the environment

recessive trait—a trait that can be hidden in one generation and then appear in the next generation

reproduction—the act of living things to produce offspring

Theory of Blending—theory that certain traits show up in offspring as a blend of their parents' characteristics

trait—a distinguishing characteristic

Index

Sally Ride Science

Sally Ride Science™ is an innovative content company dedicated to fueling young people's interests in science. Our publications and programs provide opportunities for students and teachers to explore the captivating world of science—from astrobiology to zoology. We bring science to life and show young people that science is creative, collaborative, fascinating, and fun.

Image Credits

Cover: Bettmann/CORBIS; p.3 Joanne Harris and Daniel Bubnich/Shutterstock; p.4 (top) Benjamin F. Haith/Shutterstock; p.4 Mary Evans Picture Library/Alamy; pp.4–5 Matt Purciel/Shutterstock; p.6 Razvan Stroie/Shutterstock; p.7 SPL/Photo Researchers, Inc.; p.8 (top) Vladimir Radosa/Shutterstock; p.8 (left) Haverford College; p.8 (bottom) Paul Reid/Shutterstock; p.9 Hulton Archive/Getty Images; p.10 (top) Pixshots/Shutterstock; p.10 Photos.com; p.11 (left) Adrian T. Sumner/SPL/Photo Researchers, Inc.; p.11 (bottom) Claudia Steininger/Shutterstock; p.12 Tim Bradley; pp.12–13 Ievgeniia Tikhonova/Shutterstock; p.13 Joy M. Prescott/Shutterstock; p.13 (right) Albert Campbell/Shutterstock; p.14 (top) Photos.com; p.14 (right) ANDREW SYRED/SPL/Photo Researchers, Inc.; p.14 (bottom) sgame/Shutterstock; p.15 (left) CORBIS; p.15 (right) Philip Date/Shutterstock; p.15 (bottom) Liv friis-larsen/Shutterstock; p.16 Leonid Nishko/Shutterstock; p.17 Tim Bradley; p.18 (top) Photos.com; p.18 (bottom) Tim Bradley; p.19 (left) Tim Bradley; p.19 (top) Photos.com; p.19 (bottom) Kuzma/Shutterstock; p.20 Ole Graf/zefa/CORBIS; p.21 BrandX/Superstock; p.22 (top) Paul Cowan/Shutterstock; p.22 Mary Evans Picture Library/Alamy; p23 (back) Courtesy of Haverford College; p.23 (top) Scott Laumann; p.23 (bottom) Oregon State University Foundation; p.24 (top) David B. Fankhauser, Ph.D.; pp.24–25 Roger Viollet/Getty Images; p.25 (right) Courtesy of Philip Meneely; p.26 (top) USPS; p.26 (bottom) USDA; p.27 Cheryl A. Meyer/Shutterstock; p.27 (bottom) National Library of Medicine; p.28 (top) Valentin Mosichev/Shutterstock; pp.28–29 Nicolle Rager Fuller; p.32 Getty Images